CW01095359

Strands of Infinity

Praise for Strands of Infinity

These are poems to be enjoyed sitting around a fire on a starry night in good company. Read them aloud, share them with friends, and let Looby's words encourage you to step out, write and share yours too. May there be many circles and starry nights when we join together and create connections through our words with each other.

Maddy Harland
Editor and co-founder, *Permaculture Magazine*

I am a huge fan of Looby Macnamara. Her profound insights and skill with the written word always touch me deeply. This extraordinary collection of her poetry takes us on a journey, reminding us of our great love for our Earth and our ability to create connection to the wonders of all life. She touches our deep emotions as she explores our common feelings of outrage, injustice and empathy that these present times bring, and brings us to a place of stillness, timelessness and personal empowerment. It reads like a good book, and is a veritable feast for the soul!

Glennie Kindred
Author, artist and editor of the *Earth Pathways* diary

Looby Macnamara's poems are soul medicine. Read them and feel the healing effect.

Satish Kumar
Editor of *Resurgence*

Our world so needs words of love and inspiration to breath us gently and fully in tune with the heart beat of the planet. Looby's poems ignite us, soothe us, stir our hearts and our souls. They call us to express our feelings, connect, imagine, act . . . They invite us to surrender, discover and be who we're deeply meant to be, at peace with ourselves and with all that is. Thanks Looby for sharing your love and passion for a better world.

Robin Clayfield
Author, facilitator and social permaculture pioneer

Looby writes her soulful poetry in a way that is heart opening and invigorating. Exploring the personal and the global in insightful and poetic ways she invites and inspires us to remember our interconnectedness. Not one to hide her own questions and enquiry on the journey, in Strands of Infinity *Looby shares her personal vulnerabilities, passions, bliss and wisdoms, showing us through her words a rich path forward to wholeness and possibility.*

Jules Heavens
Facilitator and founder of the *Keepers of the Flame* mystery school for women, writer, and a *poetry as medicine* carrier

Strands of Infinity *is a journey of words to nourish the soul: secular prayers of sacred eternity; songs of remembering, of loss, gratitude and joy; visionary mouthfuls of encouragement, freedom and possibility that remind us what it is to be fully human.*

Lucy H. Pearce
Author of *Burning Woman; Moon Time; The Rainbow Way*
Founder Womancraft Publishing

Looby is a voice to listen to and savour in these times. She invites us to step more deeply into our joy, passion and courage, embracing the adventure of playing our part in the larger life we belong to.

Chris Johnstone
Co-author of *Active Hope* and author of *Find Your Power*

Strands of Infinity

Poetry to Reconnect

Looby Macnamara

Strands of Infinity: Poetry to Reconnect
Looby Macnamara

Published by Greyhound Self-Publishing 2016
Malvern, Worcestershire, United Kingdom.

Designed by Looby Macnamara and Dana Wilson

Printed and bound by Aspect Design
89 Newtown Road, Malvern, Worcs. WR14 1PD
United Kingdom
Tel: 01684 561567
E-mail: allan@aspect-design.net
Website: www.aspect-design.net

All Rights Reserved.

Copyright © 2016 Looby Macnamara

Looby Macnamara has asserted her moral right
to be identified as the author of this work.

The right of Looby Macnamara to be identified as the author
of this work has been asserted in accordance with
Section 77 of the Copyright, Designs and Patents Act 1988.

This book is sold subject to the condition that it shall not, by
way of trade or otherwise, be lent, resold, hired out or otherwise
circulated without the publisher's prior consent in any form
of binding or cover other than that in which it is published
and without a similar condition including this condition being
imposed on the subsequent purchaser.

A copy of this book has been deposited with the British Library Board

Cover Design Copyright © 2016 Looby Macnamara and Chris Evans

ISBN 978-1-909219-41-0

Dedication

These poems are dedicated to my ancestors
for their wisdom and efforts,

and to seven generations of descendants;

my children Shanti and Teya,

my unborn grandchildren,

great grandchildren,

great, great grandchildren,

their children,

grandchildren,

and great great grandchildren

may they all live in a harmonious and peaceful world.

Contents

A Single Strand of Infinity. 1

Soul Medicine 3

All is Poetry 4

Dance 6

Fertile Soil to Grow a Dream 7

Messages on the Breeze 9

Giving Thanks. 11

In the Mind of a Child 13

Reconnecting 14

Will Humankind Survive? 16

I Feel You Mother Earth 18

Growing Home 19

Rivers of Pain 20

Clenched Womb 21

Danger Lives So Close. 23

What Colour is My Rage? 25

This Woman is Rising 27

Not a Drop 28

Cultural Emergence 30

Gratitude as an Attitude 33

Pivoting on the Edge. 35

Molecules 36

Worlds Together 37

The Hunger and the Longing 38

Stories Beyond Language 40

Effortlessness 41

A Whole and a Part 42

It Was You. 43

Take Off 45

Change the Story 46

Shelves of Dreams. 47

Resistance 48

Don't Play Small. 50

Arrival. 51

Magic 52

Turning Together 53

Empowerment 54

Love Letter to the World 55

Who Am I? 56

Welcome Home 58

Notes 61

Acknowledgements 62

About the Author 63

Strands of Infinity

A Single Strand of Infinity

A single strand of infinity
pushing forth
bursting into unravelling
holding all in one

and then
into nothing,
complete.

Poems weaving into dreams
mind busy with metaphor and song
eyes heavy
unwilling to open,
thoughts light and jumping
unwilling to close,
words stir my dreams

insistent on being known.
My breathless fingers find paper
connecting thought into physical
and once more release.

Momentarily into the void
before diving into the ocean of imagery
words piled high
stacked precariously
until one falls onto the page
and once more release.

Past
Present
Future
Dissolving into the ocean waves,
all that I am holding
held elsewhere,
my hands free to feel the words,
each one a doorway
unlocking a part of me,
entering through I marvel at the sights,
bewitching jewels
rarely held up to the light.

Finding rhythm,
polar bears footsteps
on crisp icy snow
crunching steadily forward,
the whole world to see
invisible below the white.
Taking a metaphor out to dance
twirling it around the tongue,
searching for the moment
when it fits just so,
and once more release.

Lying spent
belly full, mind empty
metaphors dissolved into pureness,
nothing left for the page,
my hands returning to silence
these words part of my starry night
and now once more my dreams
and now once more to dive.

Soul Medicine

Poetry as medicine
Words as arrows
Spearing through the layers
Tugging at distant messages
Finding solace in the paradox

Shifting sands of music
Mantras to my soul
Soothing
Or filing away the sharp edges
Removing persistent stains, gently

Wearing down my resistance
To my divinity.
Lines of poetry
Travelling to places words can't go
The dancer in the dance

Moving to be free.
Reaching into my healing,
Lift me out of my rut
With a phrase of beauty
So exquisite it cannot be ignored

Words calling to my braver self
Whispering their medicine to my soul
Transforming my path.

All is Poetry

The morning, the night,
the decision, the indecision
any moment of time
ready to pour its story
onto the page,
to share insights
hidden to those
focused on the next moment.

Symbols expressing my appreciation,
the warm feeling in my heart,
no ordinary words will do this job.
I'd like to share my thoughts of bliss,
reaching into delightful feelings,
excitement and calm sharing the same table.
And how else could I reach into my grief
and return more whole?

My relaxation,
a friend's dance,
seedlings emerging from the moist soil,
all are deserving of their time
in poetic motion.

I become the tree, the bird,
the moment of ecstasy,
the leaves blowing in the stormy night,
the pulse of the beating drum,
from here my belly can write its truth
vibrations expressed in language
the heart reads.

And to the questions
that never go away
Who am I?
Why am I?
I know how long my intestine is,
but how deep is my soul?
Poetry sees behind the veil
and flashes its wisdom
like lightning.
Gone –
before I start counting,
followed in five seconds or five years
by a thunderous roar
stirring my foundations.

But not everything needs to be caught in a poem
we can leave life to slide into
its own rhythmic heartbeat.

Dance

Dance into the surrender of yourself
Dance into the extraordinary strangeness
Of the freckles of your arms, like stars
Constellating in the sky, luminous flight so still.
Dance the freedom of the body escaping into itself
Dance as you once knew
Dance as you have never known
Dance as you have never been known
Dance till the sweat washes away your habits,
Liberating the tight skin around your heart
Dance until time stands still
Frozen by the movement of ecstasy
Dance the laughter into tears, so one
Contains the other and neither exist
Dance the contortions of the mind
Dance freedom shaking from rigid bones
Dance with your mind in your knees and wrists
Dance with eyes closed balanced on one foot,
Until all you can do is spin
Dance the music into your cells,
Nourishing and watering the parts in drought
Dance and play and play with the seriousness of notes
Gracefully combined together
Dance with another to feel the joy of communicating
Without words, boundaries fuzzy.
Dance, dance, dance.

Fertile Soil to Grow a Dream

Waves of poetry washed through my being
willing me to look deep into the world
for reflections of the unsolvable mystery
of myself,
of the time when I was not of my body,

When all could be seen
with eyes ready for listening
and ears open to beauty,
expressions of inspiration
shown in a word or a phrase
exquisitely dropping onto the page
to connect with others already birthed.

Weaving an exceptionally delicate story
images shimmering,
the holographic nature
eluding my mind
reaching beyond conscious thoughts
to the place of feelings and knowing

And unknowing,
of answers to questions that cannot be asked
and reaching still deeper
searching for somewhere to land

Fertile soil to grow a dream,
to shift an illusion
into a line of poetry
that can absorb mysteries and song
to share music of life
and dance with the elements inside.

A way to reach beyond words and time and space
to another luminous being
and feed the deep longing within every one of us,
to belong and understand
and to feel the spirit of humanity
binding us together.

Messages on the Breeze

With stories we link our past to our future
through spirals of time
non-existent in the moment of imagery
floating through our hearts.

Journeying with us into our lives
awakening us into our lives
awakening seeds of hope,
mystery rippling into bodily sensations
stirring the liquid of our souls.

Stories to grow through the cracks
of our culture
to bring birth to new ideas and ways of being,
our ancestors whispering lessons to our imagination
for us to play and live these stories
and turn the mundane into the sacred.

Stories to step into and shape our future,
voices of animals, plants, sun, moon and sky
translated for us
simple messages on the breeze arriving
transformed through the alchemy
of the fire of storytelling.

Reawakening the possibility of understanding ourselves
reawakening the dreamer within,
doorways into unseeable worlds
entry only through flight of dreams.

Storyteller talking through her heart
living her words
as story and person become one
and help each other grow.

Giving Thanks

I am thankful for the meaning I have in my life
I am grateful for the air that sings through me,
the breath we each breathe in turn.
It is a joy to be understood with just a flicker of eyes,
to be able to share in the fun of being human and
laugh with friends,
to bring my voice together with others in song
of such deep connection
that I don't know where my sound ends and yours begins.
I am blessed with being able to watch the moon rising
with women who understand my path,
women who relish in howling and chanting and
expressing their appreciation of her irresistible
silver light and beauty.

I am thankful for food that fills more than just my belly,
food that connects me to the wonder of creation
and to people's ability to create wonder,
to see the best of humanity and the Earth on one plate,
to share in the simple and profound pleasure of eating
from the land on which we are living.

I am thankful for the fire that warms my home
and the fierce belly fire that heats my passions.
I give thanks to the clear water flowing inside my cells,
the same life force, cascading down waterfalls,
rushing through rivers, opening to lakes as vast as the sea.

I am thankful for the family and friendship ties that take
my roots across oceans of time and space.
My heart glows and stretches to
contain the uniqueness of my children,
to embrace the miracle of birth and perfection.
I give thanks for their present sparkle
and their future dreams,
And for their ever present knowing
of how to be themselves.

Life surrounds me with its gifts to be thankful for
when I look with an open heart.

In the Mind of a Child
(by Teya Macnamara-Evans aged eight)

Thank you Earth for everything
All the things in life,
Just a few things left to ask.
Can we stop wars and
Fighting, get the homeless homes,
And make the ill better?
Otherwise I shall never get
Any sleep on those cold winter
Nights, thinking about the poor homeless
Lying out there in the streets,
With only rags for warmth.
I shall not be able to enjoy
Playing with my friends and family
For thinking about the ill who can
Only lie in bed all day.

But still life is pretty
Good.
There are a million things to be thankful for,
Butterflies, wildlife and forests,
Cats, dogs and horses,
Home and a warm bed,
Family and friends,
Books and school,
They all make me feel happy and joyful.

Reconnecting

Reconnecting with my joy for life
I appreciate being alive in this time
I feel gratitude for the wonders around and within.
As I sense the timeless beauty expressed
In the heart of a daisy
I reconnect with the radiant beauty
Travelling through the centre of my eyes.

Reconnecting with the splendour present in
Every humming insect, in every bird in flight,
In every whispering of the leaves,
I touch the icy fear present in me, that one day
These treasures will be lost from our world.
Reconnecting with the well of sorrow that lives
Inside my belly and travels so deep,
My endless tears mourn what we have lost,
And my desire to protect is awakened.

Reconnecting with my anger for all the injustices
I feel a surge of courage to make changes,
Diving below my numbness bar, I discover I care deeply
For every person and being,
A part of me shares the suffering of those
I have never met.

Reconnecting with my feelings more of myself is engaged,
I feel energized and ready to stand and make a difference.

Reconnecting with my belly I understand my power,
Reconnecting with my feet I feel my roots softening
Into the Earth,
Reconnecting with my mind I experience my edges
And my lack of edges,
Reconnecting with my heart
My love widens to fill my whole breath,
Reconnecting with my core
I am who I am and I am fluid.

Letting go of the stories of my life,
I reconnect with the poetry of my being
The intimate expression of my soul,
The Mystery held in paradox.
As I let go of the shields protecting me I open
To my vulnerability,
And in my vulnerability lies my source of strength.

Opening my eyes to the challenges of our times
I welcome the possibilities and
Opportunities for change and growth,
I reconnect with a fuller vision of what is possible
For myself and the world,
Reconnecting with strands of life
Woven between generations,
I feel myself as part of the community of all life,
Reconnecting with the reassuring presence
Of the Milky Way,
Time and space stretch and I know not what to expect.

Reconnecting with self and collective responsibility,
I realise we are too powerful not to make a difference,
I find the courage to take a step forward.

Will Humankind Survive?

Will humankind survive?
One species
Just one species amongst so many
One species, 7 billion individuals and counting
One species that think we are in control,
Masters of our own destiny
Driving the car over the edge of the cliff
Taking innocent passengers with us.

Seven billion named individuals
Several million unnamed species
Lost before they even entered the record books
Who will stand at their grave and grieve?
One loss leading to another
Spreading faster than wildfire,
Like bickering amongst children
But where is the mother to bring peace?

Warm winters, cool summers
Flooded fields and melting ice caps
Famers' suicides and stranded polar bears
Disrupted weather and ruined crops
Instincts questioned and habitats questionable

Scientists predictions too scary for newspapers
We are on the runway to runaway climate change
Each plane that ascends testament to our denial.

The economy is growing as the forests are shrinking
Faster and faster to bigger and brighter
Faster and faster to more and more
Faster and faster to less and less

Unless
We do our best.

I Feel You Mother Earth

I feel you Mother Earth
In my heart and in my breath,
Your beauty and your depth.
I try and look away
From what's happening
It's too painful to see.
I want to look away
To not believe it,
I want to look away
From people ripped from their homelands
From the land bare of trees
From the holes in your breast filled with rubbish,
But I see it
I feel it
The pain
The trouble
The destruction
And looking brings me closer to you.

Growing Home

Homegrown rage, sitting in a cage
Freedom trapped
It's just not fair
Polar bears,
Ice caps melting
Dissolving
     Collapsing
          Evolving
               Forgetting
Every pain inside
For all that hurts on the outside
Genocide
     Ecocide
          Suicide
I am beside myself
I am beside you
Next to all the daughters, sons, mothers, fathers
We are all connected
It is in this one home we live and grow
We are breaking the world
We want to remake the world
We want to remake our home
We want to grow our home.

Rivers of Pain

I take off my masks
And hold myself
As I break into a million pains
Aching in every memory,
Every moment
Unwinding my soul.

I don't want you to know
That sometimes my grief will not stop
It lasts too deep
Too many layers
Too many strands
To this thick tapestry of sadness I stand upon.

Rivers of pain bleeding into every shuddering breath.
And this hole inside of me
Stuffed full to bursting
Trembles with life
And the mystery of death.

I need to walk on the other side of my emotions
Underneath my sorrow
And on top of my joy.
The joys and pains of life
Come wedded together
And pull me apart
Into the tiniest and most magnificent self
Glistening with tears.

Clenched Womb

Every bit of her being raged
And raged and raged
In silence she screamed
Underwater she screamed
From her toes she screamed
From her clenched womb she screamed

We want to say NO
Loud and clear as a bell
So he gets it.
He gets that he crossed the line
He gets that he was wrong big time.
How can we disarm his ability to trample boundaries?
Permanently?
He let a bomb off in your life.
For every women and girl we will speak out
Right here, right now
We will break the chain of violence.

Hearing what happened
Your pain becomes our pain
And joins the pain of generations of women.
It doesn't matter what you said or didn't say,
What you wore,
What you did or didn't do
It shouldn't have happened.
He shouldn't have stumbled into your life
And ripped your innocence to shreds
Did he not think?

It's incomprehensible.
And now there is the duty of challenging him
To ensure it will not be repeated.
We need to challenge the whole system that created him
And every other 'him' that has wronged in this way
And left a devastated psyche behind.
The decades of picking up the pieces
From that one fateful night.

Talking and sharing can untangle us
from the prison of memories
Knowing he will forever be inside the walls of his thoughts.
Let's take heart from youthful ease
That breathes and lets go
Allowing experiences to fade like pencil lines.
We too can learn to be light hearted
And free from these traumas
At first only faking it
Mirroring with no inner conviction,
But slowly it takes root
Wounded wombs unclench
And we can walk free of the past.

Danger Lives So Close

I don't know where to go to scream
And ask how is this possible?
How can we live in a world where children are not safe?
Where mothers cannot trust?
I'm in shock and fear to know
Danger lives so close
In my town
In my world.

How can I open to my complete vulnerability and
hold myself in my strength?
How can I protect myself without living behind armour?
How can I warn others without spreading fear?
How can I trust and be safe?
How can I teach my children to be open and to close
themselves when their instincts warn of danger?
How can I speak out against these crimes and
keep the confidence of those in pain?
How do I stay connected to my joy and
not turn numb to my rage?
How can we stop this chain of pain?
How can I keep my ears open to hear the horrors
of your story and not traumatise myself?
How can I not sit in judgement
whilst not allowing any excuses for this hideous offence?
How can I empathise with your anguish
and distinguish your troubles from my own?
How can I face my own shadow
and see the ghost of myself in the shadows of the world?

How can I let the tears flow
and still be thankful for life's journey?
How can I soften into my fragility
and prepare myself for challenges ahead?
How can we turn this brittle experience
into a lesson of recovery?
How do I find answers and ask more questions?

Question after question falls
pitter patter, pitter patter,
building and building.
How to direct this flood
and pull the tide in the direction of healing and silence?

What Colour is My Rage?

What colour is my rage?
What colour is my grief?
I know they are there
inside of me, ready to bubble over when uninvited.
But now when I want to travel there,
when I want to explore them
I cannot find the way,
they have turned to ice
emitting no smell for me to find my way to them,
frozen by fear of being uncontainable,
frozen by the fear of falling into the icy water
and not being able to climb out,
I do not know how strong the current will be
beneath the thaw.
Can I take the risk of getting washed away?

This frosted pool of my emotions
Tugs at my thoughts, seen only once removed,
I cannot lay my heart directly on them.
I want to pierce through the shell of numbness
and descend into the shadow of my own being
to allow it contact with something much larger than itself.
It will come in the night, creeping silently upon me
when words run out of meaning,
and I find myself wandering through
the darkness of the night
tossing and turning,
tossing and turning.

This tightened knot in my gut
shows me a way in
and I am no longer skating on the numb surface
but plunging...

Instead of the unbearable depths of grief expected
and rage that explodes through my body and throat
I find the connection with a deeper channel
of beauty and light
has flowed through this place already
unseen by me,
only felt in the clear resounding tones of my depths.
This current of grace has swept away my rage and grief
leaving a dynamic peace,
and transformed the ice into
a crisp layer of power, resolve and trust.

This Woman is Rising

This woman is rising out of the ashes
Into the brightest of flames
This woman is rising into a roar that fills her crown
This woman is rising to say NO to violence against women
And to say YES to our strength
This woman is rising to tell her story
and to rewrite herstory
This woman is rising to connect with herself
And to be her full self
This woman is rising to be with sisters of every colour,
From every country, to be a global community
This woman is rising because it is essential to the world
For every one of us to rise
This woman is rising because she was hurting
And to take away the pain
This woman is rising to walk her own path
This woman is rising because she has the opportunity
And to welcome the possibilities
This woman is rising for the One Billion
This woman is rising to feel her joy, to feed her passion
And to dance for freedom.

Not a Drop

Not a drop moves inside of me,
the stillness overflowing my muscles
shuddering, shaking, stirring
until all is movement
and nothing is the same as it began.

The flow is redirected
and the dam breaks
my tears, my laughter, my excitement
mingling, brewing a magic potion
a medicine of growth
a medicine of emptiness
that exists in every breath.

Not a drop moves this river
not a drop just an ocean
between the pebbly shores of yesterday and tomorrow
the icy cool freshness of today
wraps around me
revitalising me
the summer sun warm on my face.

Not a drop of me that cannot respond
that isn't alive to the beating heart of the Earth
Not a drop that wasn't born from the fire,
that doesn't breathe the same life as you,
the same air travels from me to the multitude
of fresh green leaves on Grandmother oak.

Not a drop of me that isn't willing to stand up
and allow my heart to speak and my toes to sing
to relax and embody my courage,
to clothe my actions with the beingness of me,
taking time to be myself in every thought
and not hold back
releasing into the edge of every emotion
flowing through.

My contribution to life not a drop
but part of a growing wave of humanity
birthing a new world.
All is given with the risk it will not be enough
the tide may not turn the vast tsunami of destruction.

We will not know the ripples of our actions
in our lifetimes
they continue across generations and continents.
We can only hope future beings will thank us.

Cultural Emergence

This cultural emergency calls for cultural emergence
A breaking through, a breaking free,
Of cultures of isms and schisms
Of gun culture, war culture, rape culture, fear culture,
Greed culture, waste culture, chemical culture,
Of corporations controlling our culture
Polluting our culture.
Peeling back the layers of oil smothering our culture
Can we connect our roots into the Earth
And reach out to fellow beings and show our care?
Can we cultivate a
Responsibility culture
Friendship culture
Kindness culture
Justice culture
Safety culture
Peace culture
A culture of innovation, resilience and hope
Can we name and create the culture we want?
Can we shift our priorities, phobias, patterns,
Parameters, opinions, assumptions?
Can we bend or bury our beliefs?
Will we?

Will we reflect, connect,
Respect the collective.
Direct our objections
To the system
That promotes disconnection.

Challenge not blame,
Name and reframe,
Shift our perspective to gain a directive
That allows us to be receptive
To the interconnected web
Vibrating with every step.

Disrupt the pattern
To awaken and challenge
And begin to unravel cords of conditioning
To release the story
And create space for visioning.
Allowing the possibility of the seemingly impossible
To motivate and invigorate
The genius inside of us.
Activate and initiate
Appreciate and celebrate
Collaborate and participate
To co-create and facilitate
The desire to germinate
And take control of our fate
Moving away from this state

Of emergency
Into a state of cultural emergence
Where we use emergence to support emergence,
With the divergence and convergence of minds
Creating designs
With the intelligence of co-operating hearts
To give us a start
On this path
Of empowerment.

To bring fulfilment
And deep nourishment
It requires commitment
To trusting the process
And opening to osmosis
Of the mystical and magical
To be alchemical
With the mathematical
For practical and logical
Action and reaction
To bring connection
And emerge the solutions
For manifestation
Of personal and global transformation.

Gratitude as an Attitude

Touching hearts together
when we speak from the quiet
well of truth inside of us,
we resonate
like strings of an instrument,
our souls vibrate as we hear from each other
the beauty, magic and possibility each of us see in the
world.

Expressing our adoration and gratitude
and giving voice to what we want to protect,
what we love,
a spaciousness opens up in our chest
and we breathe in wonder
at the vastness of human capacity,
the incredibleness of nature,
the forests and trees,
the sea beds and coastlines
and the nature within our bodies.

Stand in awe,
feel the roots of appreciation
extend deep into the Earth,
draw nourishment from our connection with all life,
and the flowering of our love opening up to the sky.
The energy of the universe flows through our veins
once the channels of thanks are opened,
currents of bliss awaken and surge
stirring the life force in our belly.

Wide eyed we take in the wonder of our bodies,
we smile at the capacity of our inner world,
our inner landscapes stretching as far
as the detail of the outer landscapes,
taking us further into and further out of the fractal of life.

Taking stock of the multitude of miracles
evident in the richness of life in this present moment,
we are released from the fear that
there will be none in the future.
We know there are already blessings
brewing in the background,
miracles on the horizon of tomorrow.
The layers of trivia encapsulating our thoughts
are cut through and a wide perspective
allows us to encounter the world in all its glory.

Turn our attention,
switch our attitude to gratitude in an instant
and be thankful for the ordinary everyday gifts in our lives,
toothpaste, running water, a park bench.
Our hearts open
and our body armour dissolves
we arrive in the presence of now,
the gift of the present.

Viewing with an appreciative gaze
our mind chatter stills.
We are here and now and we are timeless.
We are uniquely ourselves
and undeniably connected.

Pivoting on the Edge

The edge is where I stand on tiptoe
with the push and pull
comes the balance
equilibrium reached through movement

and tension,
no balance in stillness
perpetual motion brings stillness
and from the depth of quiet

comes the unknown
the bottomless well of not knowing,
falling, falling, falling
and never moving from this point

of bliss and joy
spiralling inward and outward
simultaneously
in balance

pivoting on the edge
as if nothing mattered
as if everything mattered,
one strand of infinity

perfect in the moment
disappearing like a puff of smoke
released into eternity.

Molecules

The breath in my lungs
travels on the wind,
in and out of person, bird and animal
in and out,
one breath travelling through all
I give and I receive.

The molecules in my fingertips
have lived before – inside the tusk of a mammoth
my hair was once a rock on the ocean floor
my heart a distant star
the water flowing through my veins
was once the blood of ice-age rivers melting into the sea.

Molecules assembling and disassembling
in the cycle of life, death and renewal
I eat the soil from crumbling mountains
and sunlight caught in the juice of a berry
the same sunlight that floods my skin
nourishing my cells
warming the fire in my belly.

Worlds Together

Smiling we connect
person to person
from different worlds
we come together
transcending the boundaries of words.
Eyes glinting
with unspoken wisdom
finding the shared chord of humanity
beating in our hearts
sister to sister
as one we are
in this moment of life.

The Hunger and the Longing

Following trails of myself
to travel to the epicentre
of the hunger and the longing.
Each breath expanding this cavern of wanting,
as it grows the urge to fill this hole in time
with action or food or words intensifies
anything to distract me from this ache.
Food can provide a temporary cure for this hunger
that doesn't come from my stomach,
but instead of silencing it can I take its hand
and watch it be?

Happy to receive no answers from it,
just allowing the hunger to be as it is.
I can be fed by the deep longing itself,
fed by the empty wind
fed by the exploration of the void,
to be still with it and not rush to fix it
to listen for the deeper longings.

At the heart of this ache
I find the questions
Who am I? Why am I here?

Can I dwell with these questions long enough to find
meaning?
A kernel of truth I can carry in my pocket
ready for those moments of doubt and indecision,
a seed I can plant in my life and watch grow
watered with glimpses of the Mystery in motion,
and one day I can eat from this plant
and it can feed those around.

But for today, for this moment, I can breathe.

Stories Beyond Language

I am the truth and the nonsense
contained within these false boundaries of language
that can only carry me so far
language that can bring us close

but not quite together
we need more than words
to hold hearts with one another
something beyond what is made by people

and when we find this magical ingredient
then we can begin to see each other
for the complexity and simplicity of ourselves

to see the twists and turns of our being

and to know these are just stories themselves,
stories that hint of a bigger past and future
stories that invite us to be a part of the same story
to land together and revel in our sameness and differences
to share the same story as the blackbird, oak and otter.

Effortlessness

When life is as effortless as breathing
the sounds come, the words arrive, the breath goes deep
and the exhale follows needing no command.
Pushing, striving can knock me out of balance
a gentle sway can create the motion of my life
allowing heart and mind to open

to possibilities beyond myself.
Allowing me to sing from my own fire
to sound from what lives inside of me
to bring the moment of peace and quiet
together with my strength and power,
in the same ocean of sound that dissolves my edges.

Breathing into the simplicity of myself
grants me a view of my complexity.
My past and future held on the knife-edge of the present,
wisdom pulsing through the twisted braid
connecting me with my ancestors
and my great great grandchildren.

I am able to flow in the rhythm of life
and listen to the sound of the leaves
and their whispered stories of
life and renewal,
of death and letting go
as simply as breathing in sunlight.

A Whole and a Part

Fires burning
Heating from the inside
The power of being human
Exposing the vulnerability
Of our interdependence,

Lineages of wisdom
Extending through ancestral stories
Our human heritage holding priceless treasures
If only we know how to speak that particular dialect
If only we open the door to the past

And allow ourselves to step into timelessness
To sense the whole and not just the snapshot of the present
The glossy photograph of modernity
Paper thin in our hands
Crumbling under the gaze of great grandmothers.
Each of us holding the universe in our hearts
Each fragment at once a whole and a part.

It Was You

It was you I saw there
Reflected in my eyes,
It was you who spoke through
My dreams
Whispering deep desires
Too secret to be said out loud,
It was you who danced in my shadow
It was you whose fingers intertwined mine,
As you led me forward into the dark moonless night.

It was you who first caged me in,
And finally let me free
It was you taking deeper breaths than me,
Following the motion with your mind.
It was you giggling hysterically,
Tears rolling down your cheeks,
Time flowing in all directions.
It was you who faced the question,
And gave no answer

You who shattered the balloon of my ambition
And you who renewed my hope.
It was you who pressed start,
And you who will press stop,
At just the right moment.
It was you who could escape
And you who held me prisoner,
You who sparked my creative fire,
And planted bubbles in my mind.

It was you who turned on the light and started to sing,
You who ran to the hills
And came down skipping.
It was you who dived deep into inner worlds
Bringing sparkling treasures to the surface.
It was you who made my heart swell
with the pure joy of life
It was you who taught me how to hold myself in a crowd
And how to walk in silence with my own thoughts.

It was you who skipped across burning hot coals
And laughed in the breeze,
You who filled my storehouse with rainbow memories
And fiery red sunsets
You who saw the glow of my future and stepped forward
You who bathed my wounds and reclothed my beliefs.

It was you, it was me, I am you
I honour all you have given
And let go of all you have taken.

And what am I doing now
To be kind to my future self?
What lifts my wings and prepares me for flight?

Take Off

Take off
Nothing
Everything
Be at once yourself
And step into the space
Between the silence
The space immersed in silence
Where nothing can be heard
Least of all those small voices inside
Least of all those tiny voices outside
Listen,
Listen to the silence of your heart
Beating,
It speaks the true language
And when nothing else makes sense
And all is confusing or confused
This is the sound to listen to
This is the gateway
To words
That transform
An ache into a movement,
A movement
That gives way
To a new beginning,
Deeper and deeper you keep moving
Stillness and silence no longer options
That serve,
Until the moment of movement
Where flight is inevitable
And you take off.

Change the Story

Change the story
That says
I can't
Open up to the possibility of
I can
Just maybe
My mind isn't right
It's forgetting
The exceptions
The times when I stretched and stepped
Outside of my comfort zone
Wonderful moments of sidestepping
My beliefs
And being exceptional
But they aren't just accidental exceptions
They are part of the story of the new me.

Shelves of Dreams

I am searching through doorways
Into a space of nothingness
Where I open another change
Another possibility
Of who I might be
In this prolonged moment,
And who I might become
In the next dance
When my feet can leave the floor
Alternating one by one
Jumping, skipping
Until the frozen moment in time
When both have escaped
And the laws of gravity are defied
And with them
The laws of myself crumble,
And I split open
And welcome
The far reaches of who I could become.
I dust the cobwebs from the shelves
Those once forgotten dreams
Put aside still breathing,
Still wanting to grow
Now they come out of suspended animation
And float
Given a chance to grow tails and wings
And take me by the hand
Following life's impulse.

Resistance

I am asked to step beyond what I know
No, not step –
A flying leap into the blue
So ready and willing to take me.

Energy bubbles in parts of me I thought fast asleep
At the sheer mention of what might be.
Can I walk through the door flung open wide?
And declare to the world
I am here
I am me.

It's time for action
Not time to shy away and hide
Pretending it isn't me
That wants to shake and prod the status quo
That wants to shout from the rooftops
"Come on everybody let's see you
Let's see your strengths
Let's see who you really could be!"

But so much resistance to showing myself
What will people think?
What will people say?
Will I be able to escape?

Do any of these things matter?
Are they all just a smokescreen
Hiding my heart
Keeping me safe –
In my box?

As soon as I ask the question
I feel the bars around me
An extra set of ribs
I didn't know I had
They don't help me to breathe
They keep me small and contained.

Energy now bubbling away furiously underneath
A golf ball lump constricting my throat
And suddenly the bars splinter into shards of air
– Gone
And I am free
Free to say yes
And leap.

Don't Play Small

Don't play small – it is a game you have grown out of
Fill every part of your being and stand tall
Stand in your truth and in your beauty
Feel the surges of power through your body
Willing you to make sense of your life.
Make the voyage to your destiny
The journey is in the travelling
Each step showing new views of yourself
Reflect and absorb the sights
Appreciate and fully embrace yourself
Your life a celebration of life
Your life a celebration of you
NOW is the time to shine brightly and soar high
Life is anticipating this of you.

Arrival

Arrival,
Anticipation, expectancy,
Stepping into the new
And who knows what delights
We will find,
Treasures inside ourselves
When we turn the corner
From our everyday being.
We see the exceptional
Becoming our present reality
Entering into a fresh world of enthusiasm and renewal
We understand these life forces lay hidden
Within us all the time,
Talking to us in our sleep
Beckoning us out of our tight boxes
Leaving clues for our waking mind
To stumble over.
And now we have arrived
Ready to be our full selves.

Magic

The alchemy of each person
Bringing golden threads
We travel from afar
Drawn by a magnetic field
Unsure of what to expect
But with a deep knowing of arriving
Somewhere special
Inside of ourselves.
Unfolding and travelling into our centres
Taking charge of the current of our lives
Steering the boat and communicating
With the river along which we flow.

Turning Together

I am standing at the point of return
My bones remember where I am going,
A place I've never been before
To the land of our heart's longing,
We are going there together
You and I and anyone who cares to
Contribute their gifts and talents
And join the Great Turning.

Empowerment

Empowered people
Ready to hold ourselves and each other
In the dance to freedom
To sing into our hearts
And discover the vibration of the universe
And the strength of a lioness protecting her cubs.
It is through the fire we walk to our true selves
To have the courage to look in the mirror
And see behind the masks,
And gaze in wonder
At grace dropping into being.

Through holding each other
We are held
With our unity we light the world with love
With our love we understand
With our understanding we take responsibility
With our responsibility we are brave
Brave to dream of the world we want
Brave to speak our dreams
With our bravery comes action
The bold and the everyday actions that change our world
And bring hope to our souls
Hope we can breathe in deeply
Hope to wake us from our slumbers
To fill every corner of our awareness
With the knowing
All is possible.

Love Letter to the World

I'm in love with you world, in love with being alive.
I love being a guest, a participant, a collaborator,
a family member of life.
I love having memories stored within my DNA of millions
of years of evolution, and memories
of laughter and warmth and friendship
stored within my heart.
I love the circles of friends and friends of friends
interlocking and overlapping,
paths crossing and people arriving
and flowing in and out of my life.
I love my inner world, ideas flowing and intermingling.
I love my family and all the rich intimacies and reflections
I love my friends and their sharing, humour and stories,
I love each person's little quirks
and unique ways of thinking and the surprises
that arise when I open to their way of seeing.
I love all the flowers, each petal true to itself.
I love listening to the song of the trees in the wind,
a thousand leaves in the choir dancing on the breeze.
I love the smoothness of pebbles transformed
by countless strokes of the sea.
I love the sheer fecundity of midsummer, nature
bursting into every nook and cranny,
reaching forth with full abandon.

I love it all, I am so lucky to be alive, so lucky to be me.

Who Am I?

I am woman
I am child
I am me
I am feminine
I am masculine
I am nowhere
I am everywhere
I am no one and everyone
I am ancestor and great grandchild
I am past, present and future
I am air, water, fire and earth
I am Mother Earth
I am one of humanity
I don't know who I am
I am body, mind and spirit
I am movement, muscles and breath
I am bone, blood and brain
I am heart and love
I am thoughts, emotions, feelings and I am none of these
I am singer, dancer, writer, healer, mover, shaker
I am a window through which I see the world
I am a womb where ideas can grow
I am a boat to travel the cosmos
I am a spiral of connections
I am energy in one place
I am stars exploding
I am dreams flying

I am sensor of currents folding in upon themselves
I am the pattern and the detail
I am the question and the answer
I am the vastness and the miniscule
I am the oneness, the everything and the nothingness
I am the universe and the atom
I am a strand of infinity
I am eternity
And I am now.

Welcome Home

Come in, welcome,
You look radiant.
Come, sit quietly with me,
Tell me stories of your journey
Pour your wisdom and poetry over me.
Let me hear of the deep whisperings
That came to you in your silence
Your words will bring insights from within me
Tell me, where do you feel the healing?
What are your dreams now?
Have they grown and stretched?
What colour are they?
You have let go of many things
You are glowing and sparkly.
Your beauty and life force is magnetic
Welcome my friend, welcome.

Notes

This Woman is Rising is inspired by the One Billion Rising campaign; named in recognition of the one billion women globally who have suffered sexual violence at some point in their lives.
www.onebillionrising.org

The sentiment of *point of return* in *Turning Together* originates from Satish Kumar.

There is a Facebook page for more information and stories about Cultural Emergence.

Acknowledgements

I am grateful to Joanna Macy, Chris Johnstone and Jenny Mackewn who have been my inspirational teachers for the Work That Reconnects. These poems are based around the themes of Work That Reconnects spiral; Coming from Gratitude, Honouring our Pain, Seeing with New Eyes and Going Forth. I feel deep gratitude for the Work That Reconnects and the way it draws wisdom and courage from each of us.

My journey into poetry has been opened and shaped by two extraordinary women, Jules Heavens and Kim Rosen. They both do astonishing work, revealing meaning in our lives and bringing us into contact with our authentic selves through poetry.

I am thankful for all the people I've sat in circle with throughout this journey; for all their wisdom, honesty and vulnerabilities. Thanks to Jon Young for collaborating and co-creating tools for Cultural Emergence.

Thank you to all the poets whose words have opened doors in my heart and mind.

Thank you to Dana Wilson, Tracy Evans, Chris Evans and all at Aspect Design for the work in editing, designing and layout and all the logistics of manifesting this book.

Endless gratitude to Chris, Shanti and Teya for all the richness they bring to my life and for their contributions, support and interest in this collection.